AF291162

Leprenzo

Leprenzo

The Spirit within Me

Laura D'Amore

Library of Congress Control Number: 2020914486
ISBN: Hardcover   978-1-6641-2263-5
               Softcover   978-1-6641-2262-8
               eBook   978-1-6641-2261-1

Print information available on the last page.

Rev. date: 08/07/2020

To order additional copies of this book, contact:
Xlibris
844-714-8691
www.Xlibris.com
Orders@Xlibris.com
817364

Prelude

I am no longer myself. My soul shares this body with another. Wanting to forget this truth, I step outside to begin my morning run. I hear the melody of the birds chirping, and the cool breeze touches my skin. The sun rays quietly wave good morning. But the ire sound of the wind wrestling with the palm trees above brings chills to my body from memory of the universal sound of *aum*. I would chant to awaken something inside that would change me forever. My story comes from a cosmic place, a place that no one will ever be able to trace, no matter how hard. This strange story and mystery will now be yours to have as I write this from my heart to yours.

Acknowledgments

I definitely want to express my gratitude to my God. He has been with me since the beginning of time, through light and darkness. I have come to know the knowledge of the glory of God and I have tasted of His goodness. I am grateful to have received a remission of my sins. I will forever retain the remembrance of the greatness of God. I will never forget this spiritual awakening that He has blessed me with and inspired me to tell my story.

Writing my story was harder than I thought and more rewarding than I could have ever imagined. This journey could not have been possible without the love and support of my husband, Vincent. He has been by my side through every struggle in this spiritual journey. He has never doubted me and he has given me the strength to endure to the end even when I was weak.

I am eternally grateful to my parents for their love and support throughout my life and especially during these spiritually trying times. They have taught me to find strength in God to give me hope when I was lost.

This work is dedicated to my children. You have made me stronger, better and more fulfilled than I could have ever imagined. I love you to the moon and back for time and all eternity.

Introduction to My Supernatural

Last spring of 2019, while vigorously meditating in a variety of different styles to experience something spiritual, a spirit came into my body through a spiritual portal in my mind. Yup, you guessed it. I am possessed by a spirit, and his name is Leprenzo. However, I am not sure that I should classify this as a possession because a possession, I believe, is a spirit or demon having total control of one's body. I am still functioning 100 percent, and I am still myself, but I am not *by myself.* Leprenzo is not a demon. That is why I refer to him as a spirit entity, and perhaps some might wonder if this is alien.

One would think that meditation could not be dangerous in any way, especially a spirit possession. That sounds absurd, right? I really hate blaming meditation alone for getting me possessed. It was actually a lot of things that I was doing *physically* through meditation that opened up this portal to another dimension.

If you are reading this book, you are either curious about spiritual possessions, or you are curious about Leprenzo and wondering what the heck is he and where did he come from. Since he came in through meditation, you're probably wondering if meditation is even safe. I bet you are most likely wondering if I am just simply crazy with all kinds of psychological disorders. The answer to that, I like to say, is, who isn't a little crazy sometimes, and who doesn't have problems in their lives? However, in this Western civilization, I would definitely be diagnosed as "crazy," but in the Eastern civilization, I would probably be considered a spiritual guru.

My purpose is to share my personal experience, which did include, obviously, meditation. Don't worry, mediation is still safe, peaceful, and great for the mind, body, and soul. All meditation methods are great for reducing stress, and they do so in many different ways. But not for me. I did not use meditation for reducing stress.

The crazy type of meditation I was doing was the recipe that opened up the spiritual portal in my mind that allowed Leprenzo to come in. I unknowingly created a perfect storm, with a whirl wind of many different spiritual practices. I like to describe what I did as beautifully mysterious and mystical with a dash of holy crap! The question is, what was my purpose for wanting to meditate in the first place? In this book, I will cover what drove me to meditate, the types of meditations I was following, and the meaning behind the practices.

I hope that I can properly explain how I was meditating and how I was doing it. I was a total rookie, and I hardly understood how powerful this kind of stuff really is. My purpose of this book is to explain in the end how all this was the key to unlocking the doorway of which he came in. I also do not want to offend any spiritual gurus out there by giving false information unintentionally. These practices that I will mention are wonderful in many ways.

My information on these practices may or may not be completely accurate since I am not a scientist, a doctor, a yogi, or a spiritual guru. This is only my personal theory of how I believe Leprenzo came in. I promise that, if you are patient, I will explain what I did to become possessed. Am I really possessed, or is this just another psychotic case of schizophrenia?

DISCLAIMER: If you are looking to become possessed, I must advise that I am not a spiritual professional on possession or meditation. The only thing I know how to do is take your dental X-rays. Yup, I was an average working dental assistant and mother of five just trying to have some kind of supernatural spiritual awakening and—*BAM!* Hello, Leprenzo.

I am pretty sure that if you try my meditation routine, an outer-world entity will not enter your body yet. This is why I'm telling my story. These practices are beautiful when done properly and with the right intention. I do not go against any belief, theory, or practice I speak of in this book. I believe these practices are all 100 percent true and accurate. The meditation alone did not get me possessed. Be patient, I will get there.

As a matter of fact, when the spirit entered my body, I had to retrace my steps to figure out what happened, and that is how I got all my awesome knowledge on meditation and the spiritual stuff I was doing. I was desperate for an answer. Here is how it all started.

Chapter 1

Go Within

In my life's journey here on earth, I have made many decisions that have made an impact in my life and the life of others in a negative way. I was clouded and covered by the actions of my own ego. I made decisions that I could call regrets, and I have displayed much anger and rage toward others. Strangely, I do not regret my choices or actions. I have always said that my path, good and bad, has brought me here to this very moment.

In the Church of Jesus Christ of Latter Day Saints, a Christian sect, we learn that we all had premortal lives in the preexistence and we were spirits of God before we were born. We chose to come to earth to gain a body to be tested and to gain knowledge. We learned that if we followed His plan, we would become like Him. Because we are here on earth and have mortal bodies, we know that we chose to follow Jesus Christ and our Heavenly Father.

So as you can see, I grew up knowing that there was God the Father, the Creator of all, and He sent His Son Jesus Christ to teach us and to show us the way. But I have always felt strongly that there was something missing or something that I needed to learn, something that was more true and complete. Unfortunately, I never lived my life searching for God and truth, even when I knew deep inside that something was asking me to *look*.

My sister, being very eclectically spiritual, always had me in awe with the experiences she would have with God and Jesus Christ. I could not understand how she was having conversations with Jesus and feeling one with God. She was at deeper level that I could not comprehend. Perhaps I could call her a spiritual guru myself. I started to get a little jealous. One day she brought me a book to read by Paramahansa Yogananda titled *The Second Coming of Christ, The Resurrection of the Christ within You*, and she told me that I needed to start meditating to "go within." She did this because she knew that I had come to end myself, and she also knew that I was wanting to seek God like her. I wasn't sure what she meant by "going within," but I said okay, and the first thing I did was I started reading the book she had brought me.

I found *The Second Coming of Christ* to be one of the most interesting books I've ever read. Never did any book come with more power and truth, and my heart was filled with great joy. Paramahansa Yogananda describes the New Testament in such an eye-opening way. It is a book with startling ideas about the deeper meaning of Jesus's teachings and its essential unity with yoga and meditation. They say it is one of the world's oldest and most systematic religious paths to achieving oneness with God and enlightenment. I reflected over and over again about this new revelation day and night.

Yoga, meditation, oneness with God? Those were all foreign to me. However, after reading the book, I became fully aware that God was not separate from us but within us and within everything around us. This was something I already believed deep inside. This book was screaming so much truth. And then a light bulb went off! I realized that Christ's teachings were not just words of wisdom but indeed pure consciousness, seeds of consciousness that each of us already carry inside. Through the process of meditation, this Christ consciousness will simply grow and develop from within. We will start to magnify all those magnificent Christ qualities of love and light that are always present within us.

This was it! This is what I wanted to do, and deep inside, I wanted to seek Him in this new way through meditation. In this book, it mentions the importance of meditation to connect with the divine and the unity and oneness with God through Isha Kriya. Isha Kriya is an ancient meditation technique of energy and breath control or pranayama. The purpose of Isha Kriya is to help you get in touch with the very source of your existence and to create life according to your own vision and ambition. Sounds wonderful, right? And it is. The sound of having oneness with God and enlightenment gave me purpose and the drive to force what I ultimately was not prepared for. Isha Kriya meditation was only the beginning of this mystical and spiritual journey of mine. (This meditation alone did not get me possessed.)

The book inspired me to explore other avenues of meditation. I guess maybe I wanted to find a shortcut to enlightenment. I could not wait to experience something bigger than myself. And well, that's what I do—I am always searching for the next big thing. Aren't you? Why can't we just be happy? Initially, my purpose was to seek God in a completely different way, an intimate way, through this new idea of meditation.

In my search for enlightenment to find oneness, through YouTube, I discovered what is called an ego death. And boy, was this an awakening in itself! And because I had been in a deep dark place of bondage, held under the powers of temptation, I realized that my ego had brought me much suffering. I needed to explore the deeper meaning behind the ego death.

The ego is nothing more than the will to suffer. I found that the ego is only a mental construct, ideas and beliefs that are deeply ingrained in us and backed up by so much emotional baggage. Somehow we unconsciously choose fear, sadness, anger, physical pain, conflicts, poverty, and sickness. We even use our fear to perceive others and the world around us, which is everything opposite of God's love.

I no longer wanted to feel these lies that I was believing about myself. I was ashamed and tired of feeling like I deserved the pain, the consequences, and the guilt. There was a huge part of me that wanted my ego and my entire personality to crumble beneath me and fall into an infinite sea. It was like my brain was a computer on the verge of rebooting. I was outdated, overused, and had many problems. My RAM could not take it anymore. There were too many errors. I needed to wipe my "drive" clean.

I felt like I was hurting God with my ego, and God seemed to speak to me from within. He was begging me to give him my shame, my guilt, and my sins. Was it true? Could it be that there is a God with a love so scandalous, so wide, so deep, so vast, so welcoming, so inclusive? Yes! And His love is all within me and you. It hit me. I realized what "going within" meant. That God is within.

Chapter 2

A Drink from the Well

So I learned that an ego death means to let go of the false beliefs we believe about ourselves and to let go of the pain and suffering. By shedding our ego, self, and false identity, we become who we are really meant to be, awakened beings of higher consciousness and one with God.

Did you get any of that? Ego death, higher consciousness? Did it all sound like gibberish? I say it all sounds beautiful. But enough with the mushy stuff for now. What exactly is "higher consciousness," and how do you achieve it?

Higher consciousness is a term often used by spiritual gurus, often used to describe an important mental state that is extremely hard to reach. This is not at all easy to define or explain. Yet to reach a higher level of consciousness was a hot and trending thing on YouTube and many New Age believers were following. I decided to jump in. So here's my wrap on higher consciousness.

We are all conscious, right? Consciousness is a state of awareness of our environment, thoughts, feelings, or sensations; in order to experience consciousness, we must be both awake and aware. So then what is *higher consciousness*?

As human beings, we spend most of our lives functioning in states of lower consciousness, which means we are primarily concerned with ourselves, our survival, and our success. Duh, it's all about us. We are all egotistical and narcissistic at some level. I figured now was the time to dump all that so I could find God.

Through meditation, chanting, and even fasting, we can feel, even if it's just a moment, that something is changed within us. We can learn to tap into our spiritual self by learning how to slow down and pay attention to what's happening in the present moment. We start to understand things we don't even consider understanding in our normal state of mind. All that seem to fade away.

Your higher self is, in simple terms, the highest aspect of you that can be attained and held in the physical body. I like to say that God that exists with in us, is our higher self. It is the part of you that knows, sees, and understands at the highest level of consciousness possible. We no longer feel separate; we experience oneness with the universal energy field. It is awareness of the meaning of existence, your spiritual essence, and of the spiritual or energetic nature in all things. It meant to experience the joy, peace, and empowerment and that I was truly a daughter of God, so I went with it.

In this profound revelation, I found that a person's energy can move and start to transform you from within. It heals old wounds, and I had a ton of old wounds. It dissolves false beliefs and illusions, which had me question my own beliefs. Was Mormonism false? Was Joseph Smith an illusion? What's the purpose of organized religion? Anyhow, they say this energy shifts you toward your truest way of expressing yourself and living your life. It is an awakening of a dimension beyond the confines of the ego, meaning we begin to question our old beliefs, habits, and social conditioning and see that there is so much more to life than we have been taught. We become spiritually awakened.

A spiritual awakening and an ego death was now a huge way for me to find *oneness with God* and *spiritual enlightenment.* It felt like it was an opportunity to be in the presence of God in such a different and special way.

Because I was already broken and overwhelmed by the weight of my sins and the deep rage I carried within, I found myself wanting a drink from the well. The well that I now believe is within each of us. I started to wonder if we were the source, the source to God through enlightenment. I quickly wanted to discover this well within. Meditation became key, and the list of new ideas got bigger and bigger, and the freshness of these new ideas had my attention.

I no longer wanted to feel unworthy of partaking of the Sacrament on Sundays. Sacrament is an ordinance of partaking bread and water as a reminder to keep the commandments. One must be worthy of partaking in such ordinances in the church. Sidenote: I do love the Mormon Church and its principles of living. It is my number one religion for feeling the spirit and learning about Christ and being humble. But going to church as a Christian was no longer enough or right for me and I was probably lacking some humility. I was beginning to question its purpose. This will probably not sound right, but in my mind, I thought if I could have an ego death, I would be leaving my old self behind, along with my sins, and become new again through enlightenment. I wasn't even sure if sins, oneness with God, and the ego death had anything to do with one another. These were just thoughts rushing through my mind. But it sure had me curious to further explore this new idea.

Chapter 3

Do I Need a Third Eye?

In my quest for enlightenment and a cure for redemption, I started searching through the best resources I know—YouTube. I discovered something fantastic: *opening the third eye and its mysteries*. Its concept was fresh and exciting and somehow even seemed supernatural, which was, you guessed it, another new avenue I wanted to pursue. How amazing it would be to experience what is beyond the laws of nature, experience the unexplainable, witness a phenomenon. Man, what the heck was I thinking? What happened to simply having the desire for *oneness with God*? Do you see how crazy and bizarre this is all sounding? But allow me to continue.

What is the third eye? And why does it sound mysterious? And why do I need another eye? Well, it is an invisible eye known as the third eye chakra, which is the sixth chakra located in the middle of the forehead. Apparently, we all have a third eye! It's also known as the pineal gland, and this pineal gland is what I believe to be the very source of this discovery that lives within me.

They say the third eye is our greatest gift to connect us to the source. It's a reminder that the universe is much more mystical than that which we perceive with our physical senses. It's through the awakening of the third eye and its corresponding pineal gland that we are able to attain an intimate connection with God.

The pineal gland is a little bitty tiny organ buried deep in the middle of the brain. Its primary function in our body is to secrete melatonin, which helps maintain a circadian rhythm when you sleep at night and when you wake in the morning. It also regulates reproductive hormones. Although it is small, spiritualists believe that it possesses the secret to deep insights and spiritual enlightenment. Buddhists and Hindus believe that the pineal gland is the mind's eye, the symbol of spiritual awakening. The pineal gland is said to represent the point at which the body receives energy from the universe that keeps our lives sustained. It's the main access point between the astral body and the physical body. Its function in the brain is essential to our very consciousness. It is a unique part of the body that holds great powers. Who doesn't want some powers? It doesn't matter what your religious beliefs or your gender are. We all have this unique and powerful third eye. The opening of the third eye or activating of your pineal gland may produce many changes in your life, and I needed change. Its complete opening connects you to almost everything present in the universe. But for most us, unfortunately, our third eye is closed and calcified.

With meditation and direct focus to the third eye, a person can activate their pineal gland and access their higher self or higher consciousness. Supposedly, developing the third eye is the doorway to all things psychic: telepathy, clairvoyance, lucid dreaming, and astral projection—all the things I was curious about. The third eye is the gate that leads to higher dimensions to connect with other realms that might exist, not to mention other astral beings that might also exist within these realms. Let me repeat, *other astral beings that might also exist within these realms*!

All this spiritual and supernatural stuff were fascinating to me. It really got me feeling like a kid, in line at Disneyland waiting to hop on a magical carpet ride. Or maybe I was about to hop on a thrilling rollercoaster that might leave me traumatized for the rest of my life.

I always had this strange fantasy that one day I would wake up with psychic abilities. Was opening the third eye going to make me psychic and clairvoyant? Is that even a normal fantasy? Will I see spirits and demons? Anyways, I was already interested in Ouija boards, magic spells, tarot cards, psychic and palm readings. Don't worry, it was only a fascination. I never really practiced any of that. However, it always seemed to be the aisle I would run to when I went to the bookstores. Looks like I didn't need magic spells and Ouija boards, all I had to do was simply open my third eye.

Opening Third Eye Dangers

Are there dangers? Is skydiving dangerous? Of course, there are dangers! But since I jumped out of a plane before and survived, nothing could scare me. But I will advise that one should not take the spiritual realm lightly like I did. The third eye is a very sensitive part of the body. Once it is opened, you will probably see things you were unable to see before. It lets you see the unseen; your eyes will be opened. You will become known to others that exist in different realms. And believe me, I have seen and felt the unseen. However, having a closed third eye on the other hand produces many negative impacts on the body, like irregular sleep, migraines, depression, anxiety, and paranoia. Looks like, either way, you're screwed—damned if you do and damned if you don't.

Nightmares after Opening the Third Eye

Many people claim to have had nightmares after opening the third eye. It is not something unusual because dreams are a part of the mind, and what you see with your third eye turns into dreams. People report seeing demons in these nightmares. Scary, right? Of course, I did not want any nightmares, but boy, was I having some demonic dreams, and I was having constant sleep paralysis. In hindsight, not fun.

But surprisingly, none of this stopped me from wanting to open my third eye and find enlightenment. I just thought this was a normal part of the awakening. I heard that one has to go through the darkness before you can see the light.

Note to self: Just in case you're anxious to open your third eye as soon as possible, you should probably inform yourself properly about what it really means and what impact it can have on your life. Just sayin'.

Opening the Third Eye Meditation and the Health and Science

If you decide to open your third eye, you must first detoxify your body. When we put toxins in our body, the pineal gland calcifies, and we lose our spiritual connection to higher energies and our oneness with all that is. A way to detoxify is eliminating alcohol, cigarettes, and other drugs or stimulants, including caffeine. You must also stop eating so much junk! That's right, no more McDonald's.

Eliminate your fluoride to decalcify your pineal gland. But since I am in the dental field profession, I definitely continued to use fluoride toothpaste. In return, I chose to eat whole foods and consume a butt load of antioxidants. I was starting to feel like a hippie, being so clean.

Opening my third eye was a two-part session:

Part 1 - During the Day

It required

- sitting in a crossed-legged position,
- focusing in between my eyebrows, and
- meditating with a mantra.

I chose to use the words "I am not the body, I am not the mind," which is the mantra for Isha Kriya meditation.

When I meditated and closed my eyes, my astral eye, I would see blue, purple, or white-colored dots in the middle of my forehead sparkling away. To describe it better, I like to refer to it as seeing a galaxy of stars within.

Part 2 - At Bedtime

Just before falling asleep,

- I would lay in bed and close my eyes,
- I would put on my headphones, and

- to activate my pineal gland, I would listen to strange binaural beats at 938Hz
- or trance-inducing sounds of shamanic drum beats to the repetitive chanting of *aum*.

To find these sounds and other awakening sounds, you simply open YouTube (it's free) and type in "binaural beats for opening the third eye," and you will see a grand list of uploads, along with the Hz sound frequency.

I learned that listening to binaural beats is a form of sound wave therapy for the brain. You listen to binaural beats using headphones. When the right and left ear each receive a slightly different frequency tone, the brain perceives these as a single tone.

Science shows that exposure of binaural beats can also create changes in the brain's degree of arousal. Listening to these low-frequency sounds, research indicates, triggers a slowdown to brain wave activity—and that may help you relax, lower your anxiety, and make it easier for you to fall asleep. However, I did not listen to these sounds for relaxation or lowering my anxiety. My mission was to find God and discover a supernatural spiritual awakening. So I listened to certain sounds to get my brain into trance-inducing state.

Below, I will explain how certain brain waves make an impact on our daily life.

Beta: Focus, problem-solving, and enhanced energy Beta brain waves are typically those we experience when we are wide awake and full of energy. You can think of this frequency as the equivalent of taking stimulants like caffeine. The beta frequency is good for generating a concentrated, focused, and analytical mind. In fact, the brain wave you probably possess while reading a book is of the beta frequency. Beta waves are fast and have a high frequency (between 15–40 hertz). At the higher levels of this range, beta waves are also associated with anxiety.

Alpha: Calmness, tranquility, and creativity

Alpha brain waves create a state of inner relaxation and are powerful ways to reduce stress and tension. Alpha brain waves are dominant during quietly flowing thoughts and in some meditative states. Alpha is "the power of now," being here, in the present. Alpha is the resting state for the brain. Alpha waves aid overall mental coordination, calmness, alertness, mind/body integration, and learning. Your brain wave will be slower and lower in frequency (between 9-14 hertz). Your yoga class probably puts you in an alpha state.

Theta: Inspiration, intuition, and dream recall

Theta brain wave frequencies have long been viewed as the doorway to the subconscious mind. Heightened intuition, deep relaxation, extrasensory perception, and vivid dreaming are all connected to this frequency. There is a distinctly dreamy and otherworldly feel that accompanies the theta brain wave. Many therapists and hypnotherapists make use of the theta frequency to tap into the subconscious mind and heal core issues. As such, this frequency is a powerful way to change limiting beliefs and do deep inner work.

Deep meditation produces theta waves, which are slower and of lower frequency (between 5-8 hertz) than alpha waves. That murky barrier between sleep and wakefulness when you're drifting in and out of sleep and those thoughts of yours that feel dreamlike and difficult to remember, that's a theta-dominant state of consciousness.

Theta binaural beats for astral projection meditation also assist to enter the hypnagogic state, which is a portal to the astral realm, which was exactly what I was looking for to experience something supernatural or spiritual.

Hypnagogic is the experience of the transitional state between wakefulness and sleep. Mental phenomena that occurs during this *threshold consciousness* phase include lucid thought, lucid dreaming, hallucinations, and sleep paralysis.

Delta: Pain relief, healing, and regeneration

The delta brain wave is experienced by us every night in dreamless sleep. It is also experienced by advanced yogis and monks who can enter the delta frequency during deep meditation. Delta is the realm of your unconscious mind and the gateway to the universal mind and the collective unconscious, where information received is otherwise unavailable at the conscious level. This frequency also assists in both emotional and physical healing, as well as enhanced immune functioning, significant stress reduction, and even has antiaging benefits. Delta waves are slow, low-frequency brain waves (between 1.5-4 hertz) that are the dominant brain wave pattern of deep sleep.

Now that I covered the different brain waves, let's continue.

Every night, at bedtime, I would lie in bed with my headphones on, my black-out mask on to block out any light from the TV, and my body completely relaxed; I would focus my attention in the space between my eyebrows, and my mind would be completely clear of thought. The pulsating and vibrating sounds in my ears of binaural beats would help induce new vivid images. The mysteriously moving geographical shapes would quickly turn into a tunnel as if I was catapulting through space in slow motion, passing by stars that appeared to be streams of light in warp speed.

These extraordinary images would have me feeling like I was no longer in my body. It felt as if I was traveling through a cosmic space, waiting to arrive at some spectacular place in the universe. As the lights in my forehead passed me by, I sometimes felt like I would soon see God from where I was lying. Maybe that is even weirder to say. But hey, how else can I describe what you cannot see in my head?

The amazement and the perplexity of what I was seeing was not enough for me to give up this supernatural quest of enlightenment. On the contrary, it was total motivating factor. Spiritualists would say that such images are thought to be the lens of our pineal gland picking up on different dimensions. Hello! It definitely looked like I was traveling in a different dimension. I could not stop looking at this cosmic field in my mind, and the more I looked, the more I believed my awakening was coming. But it seemed it could not come fast enough.

Chapter 4

I Am Not the Body, I Am Not the Mind

After reading the book *The Second Coming of Christ* by Paramahansa Yogananda, I decided to start my day with Isha Kriya meditations by following the videos of Sadhguru who is an Indian yogi and an author of many books on enlightenment. I would follow his instructions on how to practice Isha Kriya meditation. I usually did this in the morning, around six o'clock, when I was still half asleep, when my brain was still in theta. I would repeat a second time at noon, when I was ready for a nap. The instructions go as follows:

Instructions for Isha Kriya

- Sit in a crossed-legged position, with spine as straight as possible.
- If possible, sit outside and face east for extra benefits.
- Keep your hands on your thighs with palms facing upward.
- Turn your face slightly upward, eyes closed, and keep a focus between your eyebrows.

Step 1

- Inhale and exhale slowly.
- With each inhale, say to yourself, "I am not the body."
- With each exhale, say to yourself, "I am not the mind."
- Repeat 7-11 times.

Step 2

- With one big exhale, make the sound *"aum"* deeply with your mouth wide open, exhaling fully into each sound. Do this as much as you like.

Note: The sound should come from the belly, loud enough to feel the vibration of the sound.

Step 3

- Sit quietly for 5-6 minutes with a slightly upturned face and keep your focus between your eyebrows, your mind's eye.

Note: Focusing in between your eyebrows is key to this whole experience.

The total time of this practice is about 15 minutes. Do not pay attention to your mind or body. Just ignore it, and simply sit there.

I did this twice a day for a few weeks, and during the day, I would remind myself that I am not the body and I am not the mind. Even during my morning run, I would chant "I am not the body, I am not the mind" to keep a tempo.

Sadhguru speaks about this philosophy as an element added so that one can be more aware of the breath. He says the breath is the basis of your life; most of us really do not even notice or pay attention to our breath. Those who become conscious of the sensations of the breath claim all kinds of transformations. The sensations are the outermost layer of who you are. But why did I make the sound *aum*?

Explanation of *Aum*

Aum is the primordial sound of the universe. It's the sound that reverberates in the entire cosmos and in every cell of our body. Paramahansa Yogananda states that the intelligent holy vibration or the first manifestation of God the Father manifests as the cosmic sound of *aum* or Amen, which can be heard in meditation. It also manifests itself as cosmic energy in all matter. When *aum* is chanted over and over and over again, it has the effect of deepening the meditator's consciousness and brings them into a deeper state of awareness. Even more than that, they say when *aum* is truly experienced, you can become one with the vibration and feel the universe as your own body.

I would also listen to prerecorded sounds with my headphones on. 417Hz is an amazingly beautiful frequency that acts as a cleansing agent for our body, removing negative blocks and toxicity from our body and mind. It gives rise to an astoundingly powerful effect of removing all negative emotions. These rhythmical sounds and chants are extremely powerful for healing and to induce spiritual awakenings.

Other benefits of *aum* include

- It purifies the environment around you because of the positive vibrations.
- Your concentration will increase when you chant this universal hymn.
- *Aum* chanting gives you better immunity and self-healing power.
- It has cardiovascular benefits and lowers your blood pressure.
- It improves your concentration and helps you focus.
- It can place you in a deep meditational state.
- *Aum* chanting produces a vibration and sound that is felt through your vocal cords and sinuses. The vibrations open up the sinuses to clear the airways.
- It can place you in a meditational state that gives you deep relaxation.
- The *aum* mantra has cardiovascular benefits. By relaxing our mind and body, our blood pressure will decrease, and our heart will beat with regular rhythm.
- *Aum* chanting actually improves your voice by giving strength to your vocal cords and the muscles around it.
- Through chanting and meditation, you can have better control over your emotions, thus allowing you to see situations with a clear and rational mind.

Chapter 5

Kundalini? Cosmic Orgasm? Hello!

The more I searched on YouTube for Isha Kriya, *om* or *aum* sounds, third-eye meditations, and binaural beats, the more YouTube would throw out new meditating ideas at me. The next thing I saw were endless uploads of something called the kundalini awakening. I obsessively started watching videos on what kundalini is, how do you achieve kundalini, and the dangers of kundalini. Even though I knew that there would be dangers (What's new?), that did not matter. I was on a mission. Plus, I figured since I am immune to all dangers (ha, ha), nothing was going to happen to me. I am superwoman! You know I'm kidding.

Eastern religions believe that kundalini is the actual energy of one's soul or *higher self.* Kundalini is the energetic component of the spiritual-awakening process. Every human being has the ability to awaken the divine kundalini, which lies dormant at the base of the spine until it is aroused. Most people never feel it and never know it is there. There may be a brief flash, lasting only a few seconds or longer, or it could last for minutes, even hours. In very few people, perhaps one in one thousand, this energy becomes aroused and activated. This can be a positive event, or it can be unsettling and disruptive, depending on whether you intended to arouse your kundalini or by accident.

According to tantra, the path of ecstasy, kundalini energy rests like a coiled serpent. When this dormant energy flows freely upward through the seven chakras (energy centers) and leads to an expanded state of consciousness, it's known as a kundalini awakening.

Why a serpent? Snakes has been respected (and feared) as a powerful representation of life force or universal energy. Historic and modern-day symbolism of kundalini energy shows a coiled serpent resting at the base of the human spine. Kundalini is also illustrated as two serpents intertwined around each other as they climb the spine. Interestingly enough, the shape of the serpent coupling is nearly identical to the design of double-helix DNA.

A widely recognized mainstream depiction of serpent coupling is associated with medicine. Sacred to cultures and spiritual practices all over the world, the symbol of the serpent spirit has long represented life, health, and renewal.

Fun fact: Kundalini is also considered sexual energy waiting to rise. During meditation, you may feel the sexual energy moving through your entire body in waves, filling and activating the lower energy centers with desire. If you meditate correctly and your brain waves reach gamma, this energy will travel through your brain, and it will feel like an orgasm in your head. They say it's electromagnetic! Now who wouldn't want to experience that? Sounds amazing! However, what comes up must come down. Y'all know that.

Once you awaken your kundalini, a vital energy will move through your body and clear out physiological blocks. We all have these blocks in our body where energy is stuck and we are no longer in flow with our mind-body connection, the universe, and our highest potential. When this energy flows up through your body, you may experience intense involuntary movements, including shaking, vibrations, spasms, and contractions. You will look like a wierdo. Fun, right? And since I was desperately trying to connect with the universe and have oneness with God, opening my third eye, I now needed to awaken my kundalini. Man, what the heck was I thinking?

Now I knew that I might experience negative side effects with awakening the kundalini. Many people on YouTube scream about the dangers of kundalini, but obviously, that didn't scare me. One of the many side of effects of this type of meditation is something called kundalini psychosis also known as kundalini syndrome. Spiritualists call it the dark night of the soul. Sounds depressing, doesn't it?

The dark night of the soul is what many mystics and religious scholars refer to as the ego death, which was exactly what I was trying to accomplish in the first place, not the orgasm in my head, although a blissful and surely a nice perk. As you know, the ego death must happen so that your soul can be reawakened.

The dark night of the soul is equally as complicated as it is simplistic. It is a paradox in its truest form. You have to embrace the darkness to find the light. You have to die to yourself so you can truly live. You have to experience great loss so you can gain everything. You have to lose your way so that you can begin to walk your true path. You must abandon yourself to find yourself. Ah man, that sounds like a beautiful poem, doesn't it?

Well, unfortunately, poem or not, many people have been institutionalized in psychiatric hospitals and treated, usually unsuccessfully, with strong medication and psychotherapy during this stage of kundalini. If you survive this dark night or kundalini psychosis, they say that with kundalini awakening comes powerful psychic abilities like precognition and awareness of auras and healing abilities. In short, kundalini can cause altered states of consciousness: heightened awareness, spontaneous trance states, and mystical experiences. Interesting enough, all similar to the third eye awakening as well.

Kundalini Instructions

To try and awaken my kundalini, I used a very powerful technique based on Kriya Yoga. This technique will not only awaken the kundalini energy, moving you toward spiritual enlightenment or orgasm, but it can also improve your health and remove all stress and unhappiness in your life. Except for the dangers and the possible chance, you might be institutionalized for psychosis. This technique is probably one of the easiest techniques to enter into a blissful state of meditation. Or should

I say misery? Anyways, I practiced this meditation at 3:00 PM every day when I was home alone in case of a sudden orgasm, LOL. Here are the steps that I followed.

Step 1 - I would sit in a crossed-legged position, making sure my spine is erect. I would focus on my breath, starting at the base of my spine, and I inhaled all the way up through the top of my head as if I was breathing up. I did this by visualizing the two coiled serpents at the base of my spine flowing up through the seven chakras, which are the energy centers of our body. I would focus the energy and visualized the serpents rising and exploding through the top of my head.

Breath obviously does not go up through the top of your head, but it is very effective when focusing on that with visualization. Breath is energy. The energy moves to the area you are focusing on. After practicing this for a while, you will start to feel the energy rising. The sensations will be subtle at first. But over time, it will become very blissful or orgasmic. So I tried this daily, of course.

Step 2 - Next, cycle your breath back down, from the top of your head to your third eye (located in between your brows), then down the throat, and to the heart.

Step 3 - Once these breathing cycles are completed (you can do as many cycles as you like, I did seven cycles), then just relax and say your desired mantra for a few minutes. And of course, I used "I am not the body, I am not the mind." For some reason, saying those words made it feel more magical and ritualistic for me.

Step 4 (optional) - I know you will not like to hear this, but you will have to refine your diet. You are what you eat! If you're trying to awaken your infinite internal energy or unleash the cosmic orgasm, power your practice with whole, healthy, plant-based foods. It makes a difference and can help determine your mindset, mood, and overall health.

How will you know if you have awoken your kundalini? I will list few signs and symptoms that I learned from other people's experiences. Everyone's body is different.

Signs and symptoms of kundalini awakening can include

- Energetic sensations like electricity in the body
- Shaking and jerking in the body, usually totally out of the control
- Feelings of cold in the body and feelings of intense heat in the spine or in specific chakras
- Waves of intense pleasure or bliss, even leading to orgasm
- Kundalini psychosis, let's not forget
- Anxiety, fear, and terror; some people may experience panic attacks
- Experiencing constant shifts in mood regardless of external triggers

Chapter 6

Am I on Drugs?

In case you're wondering, I do not take drugs of any kind, ever! I am completely against drugs. However, it is not my intention to judge the use of drugs. Don't worry, I do, however, fancy a little wine and beer. I am mentioning this because I read that some people use drugs to experience higher levels of consciousness than what the everyday life seems to offer. They are bored, and they are looking for a psychedelic trip. Other people have been using drugs for spiritual awakenings, personal development, and the ego death experience. But not me. Taking drugs is never an option.

When I say drugs, I am not referring to cocaine, methamphetamines, or heroin. These are dangerous substances and have very little to do with spirituality. The substances I am referring to are psychedelics drugs, such as LSD, magic mushrooms, or DMT. But it is DMT that I want to talk about because I was unknowingly producing this chemical in my brain naturally. I will explain how shortly.

DMT stands for dimethyltryptamine (don't worry, I can't pronounce it either). It's a hallucinogenic tryptamine drug that you can find naturally occurring in many plants and animals. People who ingest this drug have intense psychedelic experiences, and that is why it is also referred to as the spirit molecule or the God molecule. DMT is also said to be involved in dreams, childbirth, meditation, and mystical visions.

When people ingest DMT and come back from their trip, they report having experienced intense auditory and visual hallucinations and an altered sense of space, body, and time. Users have reported experiencing altered states of consciousness and profound spiritual experiences of traveling outside of the body. They have also reported visiting other dimensions beyond the universe or realms of existence.

Can you produce DMT naturally in the brain?

The pineal gland can actually produce DMT naturally in the brain. Humans produce DMT naturally during spiritual practices, such as chanting, prayer, meditation, and it is even said that it is produced during the birth and death processes.

I looked for ways to activate my pineal gland, and without even realizing it, I was actually producing DMT naturally. Some of the things I did to produce it was changing my diet by eating as clean as possible, I did lots of running and lots of yoga, and I made sure I had plenty of sleep. But one of the key things I did to unknowingly activate DMT was by practicing controlled breathing or pranayama, which are fast rhythm and strong abdominal contractions to expel the breath.

I would practice forced and quick breaths using my abdominals to push the breath up and down the spine and to the top of my head. After only two weeks, I found find myself in some kind of trance. Or another way to put it, I was probably astral projecting, which is the separation of the astral body from the physical body, having an out-of-body experience, traveling freely wherever you project it to go.

They say that DMT, whether it is drug-induced or produced naturally, is the doorway, key, or portal into other dimensions, which they sometimes describe as "more real than real." Some people report mystical experiences of cosmic consciousness, unity, and oneness with the infinite source of life itself, God. For these reasons, DMT has been nicknamed the spirit molecule. But here's the kicker.

Many people report having experienced contact with otherworldly intelligent entities. (Hello!) The question of DMT and aliens is one that deserves real consideration, please!

Given that this bizarre chemical in our brain can invoke some kind of "entity contact," regardless of age, gender, language or religion, could there be something to the idea that these entities are actual spirit beings? *Aliens*, even?

So did I ingest DMT? Hell no! I don't take any type of drugs unless prescribed by my doctor. My theory about my own personal mystical experience is that I was producing DMT naturally by using the breathing techniques during my meditation. The act of inhaling from the base of your spine and pushing that breath all the way into the brain and holding your breath, you exert pressure against the pineal gland that may produce a certain chemical in the brain. I believe that chemical was DMT because it seemed to produce the same mystical experiences that the psychedelic drug substances produce.

Chapter 7

3:00 am

So in the end, Isha Kriya meditation, oneness with God, repentance, ego death, the third eye, binaural beats, kundalini, spiritual awakening, enlightenment, and the supernatural were all the ingredients that drove me to create the perfect spiritual storm. Sounds like sorcery, doesn't it? Maybe I'm a wizard after all and not superwoman. I am feeling ready to get my holy moly supernatural on and start this old age and new age practice. Where's my yoga mat?

Now comes the fun part: the consistent but not consistent, my invention, the all-over-the-place recipe that opened the portal that got me possessed.

Sidenote: I know that sometimes I sound lighthearted and happy about all this—you know, about being possessed and all that. Or maybe I even sound funny or humorous. But I have two options with regard to this: I can live in fear or live God's grace. I choose God and happiness, with a touch of I'm F-ing pissed. (I'm not holy or perfect, only human.) This possession, no doubt, is overwhelmingly real and true. The reality of my situation has brought me to my knees with questions, pain, fear, and anguish. At the same time, I have had moments of joy with the discovery of what's inside me, which you will find later.

Sometime in April of 2019

My meditation practices soon became an all-day thing: morning, noon, and night. I woke up meditating, had midmorning meditations, afternoon meditations, and bedtime meditations. With all the meditation sessions, I would clear my mind completely, and I would focus in between my eyebrows to witness the phenomenon within. During the day, I would wear a black-out eye mask to avoid the daylight and to avoid any sensory distractions from the outer world. I took this very seriously, and I was completely engaged in my practice.

6:00 AM was for Isha Kriya meditation, 30 minutes

9:00 AM was for breath work and chanting mantras, 30 minutes

11:00 AM was for basic guided meditations to open the third eye, 30 minutes

3:00 PM was for kundalini activation, breath work, and visualization of uncoiling the serpents from the base of my spine through the top of my head, 30 minutes

8:00 PM was for listening to binaural beats for opening the third eye and astral travel projection at 936Hz and listening to *om* chanting at 432Hz, 1 hour

I followed this routine and schedule for four weeks, and then things started happening. The first thing that I noticed was an obvious pulsing in my head when I meditated. I could rarely find stillness in my meditation anymore because as soon as I closed my eyes, there was a sensation of a heartbeat beating in my head. I was deeply surrounded by this whirlwind of pressure, throbbing and pulling all at the same time. The constant motion and jostling was like a rhythmic chaos that pulled me forward and backward. I assumed this was all part of the process after reading the signs and symptoms of kundalini awakening and third eye opening. I would watch people meditate on YouTube move slightly forward and back just like I was. Sometimes it looked like their bodies where having seizures, bouncing and shaking all over the place. So this seemed normal to me. But this was only the beginning of my supernatural experience.

A few days later, the same strange and strong pulsing in my head woke me at 3:00 AM. The pulse was like someone or something was knocking at my door, not my front door but the astral door within. It obviously woke me, and with curiosity, I quickly turned to my back and closed my eyes to see what was happening between the space of my forehead. And just like that, the stars and shapes that I was used to seeing suddenly came together before my eyes into a perfect mystical circular medallion containing lines of electronic rays in the middle of the dark space between my eyebrows. The glowing halo in the middle of my forehead looked like the iris of our eye in a beautiful electric blue color. In the very center of this eye was a dark tunnel that looked like the pupil of our eye. Holy cow, was I staring at my very own third eye? Or perhaps a portal to a different dimension? Should I have been scared? I don't know. My first thought was that I wanted to wake my husband up to show him what I was seeing! But no, I quickly realized and remembered that this unexplainable sight was in my own brain and no one can see it. As my consciousness was waking from the wonderment, the eye started dissolving back into the little moving stars and particles, of which I like to call the galaxy within.

The very next morning I could not stop thinking about what I saw in my head. The night could not come soon enough. When it was finally bedtime, I put on my headphones and listened to different frequencies to activate my pineal gland in hopes of seeing what I thought was the third eye again.

About three nights later, approximately at 3:00 AM, I was once again awoken by the pulsing heartbeats in my head. There it was, the mystical doorway shining bright as ever. I am using different words to describe what I saw because I will never know the truth of what it is. Is it a doorway? Or is it my third eye? It looks like an eye, but it also looks like a circular opening to another world. Whatever it is or whatever it was cannot be explained. All I know is that I knew something was happening within.

In the mornings, after my run, I would get my yoga mat and go out to my courtyard, and upstairs I went. We have an upstairs stargazing patio that I would use privately to meditate and chant. During my 9:00 AM session, I would sit in a crossed-legged position and bring my hands to prayer position, heart center. Then in one long inhalation, I would bring my hands up above my head, bringing the hands together, and back down to heart center once again. After a few breath cycles, I added my mantra of choice, "I am not the body, I am not the mind." I was in the zone, probably in the alpha zone, getting my Zen on. After a few cycles of that mantra, I would begin a work by calling on the universe by chanting *aum*. I did a few variations of that sound. The chant mainly sounded like I was reciting my vowel sounds. In one long exhalation, I would say, "Aaaaaum." The sound was deep and coming from my belly until my breath went completely out. Then I would repeat with "ooooooh" and "eeeeeeeeee." While I was seemingly feeling like I was having an outer-body experience, my pineal gland was also in rhythm with the chanting. There was something special about what I believe was an awakening from within. My body was circling, and I was in rhythm with the source. I was literally imagining at that moment that my ego was falling away; nothing in this world even mattered. At least that is what I thought was happening.

Sometimes the cosmic powers of the sound and meditation felt like I was making magic. The possibilities of the supernatural were near and close. Or was it already happening? I could feel my mind transcending and illuminating with glorious hope that I was also starting to connect with my higher self and feeling one with God. I couldn't wait for bedtime to resume with the binaural beats to further open my pineal gland. Was I astral traveling? Was I in a different realm? Was this real or an illusion? I guess I will never know.

A few nights later in bed, while doing a guided meditation, with wonderment, I noticed in the space between my eyebrows a bright luminous outline of a face drawing nearer to me. As it slowly seemed to get closer, I felt myself sweating, and a dash of fear started to creep in. I did not want to stop looking though. When the face came to a halt before my eyes (my astral eyes), I stared long enough to notice the structures and the outlines of this wonder before me. There was something familiar about this face; her almond-shape eyes were closed, the lips of her small mouth were closed, and the nose straight and narrow. I realized that the face I was looking at was me. The contours and the shape of this face were the contours of my own face. Was I embarking on something spiritually wonderful or spiritually dangerous? Is this even normal? Do I need my eyes checked? I need answers!

As I looked upon this neon face that stared silently back at me, I wondered if this was my own spirit, my soul, or my higher self. Or could it be a visitor from another dimension creating an image of my own face? Or was this my spirit guide? I didn't know. This new mystical experience before me was nothing that I was even prepared for. Nothing I read ever spoke about the things that I was witnessing in the space between my eyebrows. I tried searching on Google but found nothing that resembled what I was seeing in the night. Even though I had no idea what was happening, the fear was still not enough to stop this spiritual journey. The fact is I wanted to experience something spiritual and something supernatural. I seemed to be traveling on the yellow brick road to meet the wizard, but was I actually on the right one? I don't know, but I continued to press forward.

Four weeks into this heavily stimulating, no drug, meditation practice, things were happening inside. On top of the astral images I was seeing in my head, I was feeling happier during the day, I was not complaining and bitching at my husband out of boredom, and it seemed like every day was "a beautiful day to be alive." I somehow believed that I was feeling connected with the divine and the infinite source of all that is. *Life was good.* So it seemed.

Another night, at 3:00 AM, the thumping in my head awoke me once again. The mysterious cosmic eye or circle had actually frightened me. *Oh my god*, I couldn't believe what I was I seeing! This time the same electric blue eye or portal that I was used to seeing had a glowing red center. Why was I seeing red so brightly like this? All of a sudden, the entire portal started rotating clockwise as if I had just unlocked a key to another world. This might not even seem scary to you, but believe me, it was. This is probably one of those things that should remain a mystery. I am not sure that God even intended us to be witnessing these kinds of things. All of a sudden, the spiritual world felt like it was not to be tampered with any longer, but the now the tides had turned. The spiritual world was tampering with me.

Chapter 8

Enter the Dragon

Questions where running through my head: Should I stop engaging in such things? Or was this all part of enlightenment? Was I witnessing the path that I will take when my spirit leaves this body? Was this a portal to another dimension? Was this my third eye? One thing I learned for sure in this process was that we are not the body; the body is nothing but flesh. We are so much more than we could ever imagine. We are energy. We are spirit. We are cosmic beings. We were divinely created by something grander, something intelligent, something that designed us so perfectly. We are connected to the divine source, but this revelation, for some reason, had me on edge now. I was kind of scared because of the unfamiliarity of what was happening inside.

As I carried on throughout the day, for some reason, my body somehow felt like it was still in another realm, per se. My pineal gland would not stop alerting me, thumping throughout the day, causing my head to pulse even when I was still. When I did everyday girl things like putting my makeup on, my body would fall into a trance. My eyes would roll back blinking quickly as if I was traveling to another dimension or becoming hypnotized, and my pelvis and head would start to do upward body rolls. (Another way to describe the body rolls is that my head was tossed back, and my body was rocking in waves.) Instead of just fighting it and saying "hell no," I simply relaxed and let it happen.

Sounds strange, but it was causing some kind of arousal within me, and I was kind of enjoying it. Was this the kundalini energy working its way up to my brain for that orgasm in the head? I guess I will never know because that infamous orgasm never happened.

After that strange but exotic feeling, I remembered that I no longer wanted anything to do with the supernatural or spiritual awakenings. Funny, surrendering to this energy was like eating a gigantic bowl of ice cream with all the fixings and then feeling great remorse quickly right after. So once again, I needed to dig up the will power to resist. But my body was constantly rushing with this unique energy all day long, and it was actually starting to become uncomfortable because I was resisting. I needed will power!

A big part of me wanted to give up the supernatural, but it seemed the supernatural had already found me. That night I went to bed feeling uneasy, but this time, by as early as 10:00 PM, my head started thumping again as usual. Even though I was a bit scared, I took a look inside to see what was happening. It's really hard to ignore the mystical things that are happening to you, especially inside your head. The human body sends warning signals to alert you when something is wrong. So of course, I had to look! As soon as I looked within, I took a deep breath, and there, before my astral eyes, was an image of a spirit or ghost slowly approaching me. The spirit was a smoky white in color, and it was in a crossed-legged position as it approached. When it finally came to a halt before me, I noticed the features of its face. This time it definitely was not me. It was male. He had spaces for the eyes and an opening for the mouth. He had no nose and no obvious ears like us. As he stared at me, I stared bravely right back at him. He then began to communicate with me by using his arms. He was doing exactly what I was doing every morning outside my patio. With his hands in prayer position, he circled his arms around and up above his head and brought his hands back together again. He circled his arms over and over and over again for about half an hour. I became exhausted from staring, and for some reason, I said to it, "Okay, you want me to go upstairs and meditate. I need to go to sleep now. I will meditate tomorrow." I closed my astral eyes and went to sleep.

By the next morning, I got my yoga mat and ran upstairs to do what I thought the spirit or ghost was asking me to do. Now why the heck would I do such a thing? Perhaps I was still curious. Keep in mind, there are many YouTube videos that say, "Meet your spirit guide." So in the back of my mind, I thought I had met my spirit guide that night. As I sat down, I began my mantras once again, bringing my hands to child's pose and circling them around and around just has he did. Then I sat in silence with my eyes closed. My head was gently thumping and my body moving forward and back ever so lightly. Maybe I was expecting something great to happen. Perhaps I was finally going to meet enlightenment. This was it!

I was completely wrong. Nothing happened that morning. But that night was a different story. That night was the night that changed my life forever. Sometime around 2:30 AM, my pineal gland startled me. It was not just thumping. This time the beats of my pineal gland awoke me with alarming speed. The thumping was so fast and loud that I could literally hear it in my head. My heart quickly joined in rhythm. My body seemed to be in panic as if I was about to meet death. As I turned to see what the heck was happening with my astral eyes, I witnessed an image of a spirit beaming with gold lightning rays all around it approaching me fast. I could literally feel my whole body sizzling as it was coming closer. I jumped out of bed so quickly as if I could escape what was coming. But it was too late. My body was no longer the same.

There was a strong layer of static covering me as if someone rubbed a balloon all over my body. I woke up my husband, and all I could do was ask him to hold me. At that moment, I did not care to explain what I had seen and felt. I wanted it all to go away. This was extremely frightening, and the funny thing is I had no idea that a spirit actually entered through my pineal gland and into my body. Obviously, I was overwhelmed, and not able to sleep that night, I decided to fill my bathtub and soak in the water in hopes for the static to go away. It felt like I was in a scene of a paranormal movie. I was paranoid, and all of a sudden, I thought that demons and ghosts were all around me. I had never felt such fear in my life.

I immediately knew in my heart that I had opened up something dangerous this time. Well, it felt dangerous anyways. At that moment, I decided this was no longer anything I wanted to further explore. The unknown should remain unknown, and I was to return to life as a normal human being as soon as possible. Human ignorance, all of a sudden, seemed blissful. I cried out to the Most High that night.

The morning could not come soon enough. When the morning came, I got up and went on with my daily life as usual, pretending that nothing happened. Once again, I thought to myself that I should not be tampering with this unknown activity. However, I couldn't help but notice the slightly uncomfortable energy building inside me. I decided that I needed resist this energy. But for some reason, after resisting all day, when the night came, the energy was too much to bear. By 8:00 PM, I could not take it anymore. I told my husband that I needed to go to the living room to let this energy out by doing some yoga. I thought maybe some light exercise would help relieve the energy.

As I sat on my mat, I decided to find some slow-flowing rhythmical yoga music to put me in the mood to do some power yoga moves. I sat on my knees, with my butt gently sitting on the heels of my feet, and I was ready to begin. With the energy waiting to be released, I pressed play for the music to begin. As quickly as I brought my head to the ground in prayer pose, the energy within quickly pulled me right back up. The pull was clearly not coming from me, but without fear, I surrendered my body to what I thought was the kundalini energy.

The energy within me took over, circling my body to the flowing music. My head went back, and my body swayed side to side gently as if a sacral dance was about to begin. For some reason, I was not afraid because of the graceful movement it was making with my body. Then all of a sudden, my arms took over in such a way that had me mesmerized. The movements were as if a ballerina took over. But this was not me at all. It seemed as if I had awoken the divine spirit within me, and it was gracefully and beautifully dancing to the rhythmical sounds.

The energy manifested itself as a female spirit or female goddess that was using my body to do this dance. Her fingers gently touched the skin of my chest, and then she grazed the skin of my face as if it had been an eternity without a body. I could sense the excitement she was feeling inside me as the dance continued. It seemed as if she was trying to tell me that she had been lost forever and now she had been found. She celebrated the gift of my body through this tantric dance.

I didn't know how to feel, I had a million thoughts rushing through my head. Was this Shakti, the kundalini spirit herself? Was this my own holy spirit or higher self? Should I be afraid? As these thoughts were rushing through my head, my husband walked in the room, and the spirit came to a halt. She stood there with a light rocking, but the dancing was over, so I stood up and asked my husband with excitement, "Did you see that?" I can't remember his response, but I'm sure it sounded something like "You look like a waka doo."

As I rolled up my mat, I felt a strange static electricity running through my body. When I proceeded to walk back to my bedroom, the static was extremely intense. All the hairs on my body were standing up. One of my cats who was watching me the entire time backed away from me. He arched his back, and his fur stood straight up. Seemingly frightened, he began to hiss and growl at me as if he had seen a ghost. At that very moment, the joy turned into fear, and I became immediately frightened once again. Something was not right, and I knew deep inside that I was in trouble. Did I have a spirit inside me? Could I be possessed?

Seeing my cat this upset by my presence made me realize that this was all wrong. Anxiety quickly took over, and without any hesitation, I called the bishop from my Mormon church. I told him that this was an emergency, and he needed to get out of bed and come immediately. He called one of his counselors, and they quickly came over. After explaining my journey that led me to this point, they placed their hands over my head and gave me a priesthood blessing. As beautiful and comforting the blessings always are, I knew it was not enough. I felt like I needed someone to act with conviction and authority to get this spirit out. I went to bed feeling hopeless, frightened, and exhausted. But the party wasn't over yet. This was only the beginning.

Chapter 9

Are You a Good Spirit?

Wanting to forget what had happened that night, I stepped outside to begin my morning run. As I heard the melody of the birds chirping, the cool breeze touched my skin, and the sun rays quietly waved good morning. But the ire sound of the wind wrestling with the palm trees above brought chills to my body. The sound of *aum* I had chanted before was still vibrating in my mind. It was clear that I was no longer the same. I was not alone anymore.

The fear of this dark idea that I was possessed was an ungodly feeling. Why was I feeling the presence of a spirit inside my body? Where did I go wrong? Was I doing witchcraft by chanting? Or did I awaken a spirit within myself? As I put on my headphones, I chose to listen to Christian music to fill my soul with the spirit of God. I prayed, "Lord, I need you now. Please be present in my life."

While I was running my problems away, all I could do was focus on my physical body. Hoping this was only a dream, I tried to determine if I really had a spirit inside me. As I was coming to the point of return in my run, my head involuntarily moved upward and back as if a horseman was pulling me with the reins. Whoa, that freaked me out! "OMG, I think this really is a spirit inside of me!" I ran home as fast as my legs would let me as if I could escape.

When I finally reached the end of my run, my heart and lungs were fully exerted, and all of a sudden, I could feel my arm vibrating with a pull. The spirit placed my hand on my heart as if to acknowledge that my heart was pounding away. The fear of the sudden truth must have scared the "shit" out of me because the spirit touched my belly and then brushed my belly from the top to the bottom and "out" as if the spirit was letting me know that I had to poop. What the heck was happening? Who is this? What is this?

As the tears were falling down my face, the spirit wanting to express concern, it made a fist and placed it right at my heart. It seemed to be expressing love and kindness toward me and letting me know that all was good. So was this a good spirit? I needed to calm down and think.

Deciding that I needed to be brave and communicate with this spirit, I walked through my house and out to my private courtyard. I sat in front of my beautiful rocky waterfall covered in palms and cacti. The sound of water somehow made it seem like a safe place to be. I sat in a crossed-legged position and closed my eyes. I spoke out loud, "I am speaking to the spirit within me. I would like to ask you some questions." Since the spirit was obviously using my body to move as it willed, I gave it instructions for communicating with me by using my body. If the answers to my questions were yes, it moved my body forward and back. If the answer was no, it moved my body in a circle. I came up with the "yes, no" idea in a pinch because of, you know, the Ouija board game. Since there was no voice from this spirit, I needed to think outside the box, the Ouija box. I began the questions.

"Are you a spirit?" Yes.
"Are you a good spirit?" Yes.
"Are you the kundalini spirit?" No.
"Are you a Hindu god or goddess?" No.
"Are you my third eye?" No.
"Are you here to hurt me?" No.
Again, I asked, "Are you a good spirit?" Yes.
"Then I am happy you are here. My name is Laura." But then the thought occurred, it probably already knew my name.

"Do you know my name?" Yes.

"May I speak with you throughout the day?" Yes.

"Can I tell my husband about you?" No.

The fact that I could not tell my husband about the spirit within me made me feel like I was a part of some covert operation. This mission was to remain unknown until further notice. Like Joseph Smith in the Book of Mormon, I thought maybe this might be a messenger sent from the presence of God, that God had a work for me to do. I was not to speak of this until further notice.

I said thank you, and I got up to do my daily household responsibilities. The reality was that I thought I had just simply woken up my own spirit or "my higher self." Man, was I stoked! My fear turned to joy, thinking that I was having a "spiritual awakening." The thought of me being possessed by an unknown spirit had melted away, at least for a short time.

Innocently, I decided to have a little fun with this seemingly new supernatural enlightenment within me. I was skipping around like a little schoolgirl because "It felt like I created magic within myself!"

The questions continued throughout the day while doing my chores, my body moving forward and back and round and round as we were communicating back and forth. I can't fully remember all the questions I asked. In hindsight, I should have been journaling from the beginning. But all I knew was that I was on cloud nine, thinking I had achieved an awakening, and I was feeling like a kid again.

I slept like a baby that night, thinking that I was in the comfort of my own awakened spirit. By the next morning, things were still the same. I went out for my run and asked a million questions, still feeling the sensations of the yes and no answers without any fear this time. When I got home, I decided to go upstairs to my private stargazing patio to have our conversation in private. My husband still had no idea what was going on, and I was careful not to do any weird stuff around him. I did not want him seeing my body move forward, back, round and round. I was not ready for questions yet.

Kneeling on my yoga mat with my knees on the ground, I wanted to ask more questions, but I didn't know what to ask any more. It was difficult because I was the only one who was able to speak words at the time. So instead, I asked the spirit if it wanted to listen to music. I remembered the tantric dance we had earlier that week. It said yes, so I played a rhythmical trance like yoga tune to feel the flow of this spirit within me. The beat of the tantric drums and the spirt flowing through my entire body felt like pure magic.

The next morning, as I was sitting in the kitchen with my husband, I felt a pull in my neck. My neck turned to look right, facing the window outside to the courtyard. The spirit did this three times, so I asked if it wanted to go upstairs. It said "yes" with my body moving forward and back. Obeying, I eagerly went out. I ran upstairs and sat on my mat. I asked the spirit if it would like to listen to music, but this time it was a "no." The spirit pulled my body down. My head was placed on the mat for some time. I thought maybe it wanted me to pray. I sat back up, and I asked if I needed to be in prayer, and it said "yes," so I placed my head back down on the ground and started to pray. My prayers were of gratitude. I prayed for everyone and everything around me. When I was finished, I sat up, but apparently, it was not enough, and my body was pulled back down. I didn't know what to pray for anymore, so I knelt silently. With concern this time, I sat up, but my body was pulled back down again. This time I stood there silently with my forehead on the mat for about ten minutes until my body was pulled to sit up.

After all that was done, I asked if it wanted to listen to music. For some reason, I really wanted to feel the spirit dance within me. I loved it! I played the same music, the spirit took over, and my arms and body flowed and danced away. I had never felt so graceful in my life, and my body had never moved to music in such a beautiful way.

We carried on as usual throughout the day. As I walked past my bookshelf that had an array of spiritual books, I immediately had questions to ask. As I held the Bible in my hands, I asked if it was true, and it said "yes." I held the Book of Mormon in my hands, and it said "Yes." I held the *Second Coming of Christ within You* by Paramahansa Yogananda, and it said yes. All three books had truth in them. I think I wanted to cry, feeling like I had just been touched by the Holy Spirit, affirming me that I was on the right path to enlightenment.

Walking around the house and doing my chores did not feel the same anymore. I could feel the constant pressure in my head and neck, and as I moved about, the spirit was curiously looking around as it pleased. It seemed so curious about the world around me as if it were the first time experiencing earth. My body was no longer one anymore. I was sharing it with another. As I walked, moved, and turned, it moved with me. It was an indescribable obvious pull inside my body.

The third day came and went. We had the same morning routine. We ran, had coffee, and went upstairs to pray. The kneeling down with my head on the ground sometimes lasted half an hour. There were moments when I no longer wanted to do what this spirit was asking me to do. First of all, it is very uncomfortable sustaining your body weight over your knees for a long time. I was losing circulation, and then when I came up to breathe, the spirit quickly brought me back down. The spirit was so bossy sometimes!

Not knowing how to feel about this constant pull and the constant need to bring my head to the ground started to make me feel uneasy. But I remained brave for the cause in believing that this was something bigger than me. Maybe it was of heavenly importance, an awakening with higher purpose. Or perhaps my "higher self" just came alive inside me, and she really needed me to pray and repent.

Chapter 10

Birthday Cake Ice Cream

Living my life as a normal human being was no longer the same. The curiosity that the spirit had of the world around was obvious. My head was constantly turning left and right and up and down to see the world and all that was in it. Going to the store was always an interesting event. It seemed like the spirit had some type of intelligent radar, and somehow it knew exactly where the item was that I was looking for. For example: One time I needed corn that was already prepped and packaged, that was a very specific item, and I barely knew the store, and all of a sudden, my body seemed to pull me in a hurry to the produce department. The corn was nowhere to be found in my sight, but the spirit wrapped around an aisle, and there stood the packaged corn.

There were many times that I wanted one thing, but the spirit wanted another. We played the tug-a-war game constantly at the store, and that had me in laughs. Of course, the spirit always got what it wanted lol.

Going shopping for clothes with the spirit was fun too. The spirit, knowing what was on my mind, would literally take me to the item I was looking for. I no longer had to search around looking lost. Shopping became quick, fun, and easy. When I was done shopping, the spirit knew exactly where to find my car. I mention this because I could never find my car in large parking lots. Who has the same problem? I was always having to reach for my keys so I could get my car to alert me. Not anymore, I could literally close my eyes, and the spirit would take me to my car. The telepathy of this spirit seemed incredible? Or was this the telepathy of the mystical third eye directing the spirit that was in me? There were so many unanswered questions running through my mind.

Another interesting event happened the day I wanted to buy ice cream. One day I was craving mint chip ice cream, specifically from the brand Tillamook. When we entered the store, the spirit dragged me up to the ice cream aisle and placed me directly in front of the exact mint chip I was looking for. As I was reaching for the mint chip ice cream, my hand and body avoided the mint chip and turned slightly to the left to pick up a different flavor, birthday cake. The spirit was clearly asking me to pick up birthday cake ice cream for my daughter Romi. Birthday cake ice cream happens to be her favorite flavor of choice. At that moment, my heart was filled with love, realizing that the spirit was wanting me to think of my daughter first. I am not a perfect mother. I lacked patience and sometimes acted out in anger. This change in direction was causing me to reflect on my relationship with my baby. It seemed the spirit wanted to guide me in being a better mother. I was humbled by the birthday cake experience.

Chapter 11

A Trip to the Library

One week into to this supernatural spiritual experience and my perspective changing minute by minute, I was still having a million questions. Not being able to fully communicate was quite frustrating. My mind was wondering if this was a heavenly being taking record of my actions. For some reason, I felt that it wanted me to repent and be a better person. I had a new awareness and desire to become a better human being while I was here on earth.

This was my first year of homeschooling Romi. Being her learning coach was tough for both of us, and I found myself losing my patience daily. If this was a heavenly being, I better be on my best behavior and start teaching Romi with love.

Our days of homeschooling now began with a prayer, reading the scriptures. Some days we would start with studying the Ten Commandments from the Bible, and other days we would study the Mormon Articles of Faith. Sometimes I would even read and study the teachings of Paramahansa Yogananda, which is my personal favorite.

School, prayer, and scriptures were now a happy event for Romi and me. School was no longer a chore. I was learning to become more patient, and my anger was melting away. We were hugging and loving each other and having fun every day. I was deeply grateful for this presence within me guiding me to be a better person. I was feeling a love that I had never felt before, how lucky I was to have this gift within me.

One morning, after her tennis lesson, as were driving home, I remembered that we had to go to the library to check out a book for her class. We were in a hurry to get home so she could log online to meet with her class. So guess what happened? You guessed it—the spirit telepathically knew where the book was, and we were in and out of there in no time.

With a few minutes to spare, we decided to open the book up to read a few pages. We got comfortable on the carpet and leaned against a comfy chair. As we began to read, the spirt placed my head on Romi's shoulder as a sign of affection. I couldn't believe how simple this was; love felt so simple. This spirit was teaching me to be loving and more affectionate, and my heart was feeling warm and fuzzy.

When it was my turn to read, my head was pulled upright with curiosity, and then something new and strange happened. My eyes were speedily reading through the pages and finished before I could even read the first sentence. My head moved up and down quickly, reading the pages as if the spirit was the computer robot Short Circuit, digesting information at warp speed. This new discovery and feeling my eyes move so quickly as they were reading through the pages presented a new concern. This was so unknown and mystical to me, and yet I knew nothing about this spirit, except that it was a good. It was time for me to figure out a better way to communicate with the spirit. I wanted to know who or what it was.

Chapter 12

The Tarot Cards

The next day I had an epiphany! I wanted to go to the bookstore and have the spirit help me find a book that would help me figure out what was happening to me. I asked the spirit, it said "yes," and off we went.

Enthusiastically, we walked into the store, and the spirit, feeling my excitement, had me walking at a brisk pace. Do you want to guess what happened next? You guessed it—the spirit already knew in an instant which book aisle we needed to be at. Knowing I had never been to this Barnes and Noble and wanting to test the spirit's ability to find things instantly, I simply allowed the spirit to pull me along as if I was the passenger going along for a ride. We reached the aisle, turned right, and of course, it was the spiritual aisle. Who would have guessed?

Taking over the vehicle now, I knew what I wanted to look for. I was looking for books by Dr. Joe Dispenza, who happens to be a doctor, a scientist, and a modern-day mystic. Thinking maybe I was becoming supernatural, I was looking for his book *Becoming Supernatural*.

But no, the spirit quickly took over the driver seat, pulled my body, walked, and then stood where it wanted me to look. My head was forced to look down, so I gently sat on my knees. Surrendering my arms, I allowed the spirit to reach for the book it wanted. I could feel the static in my arms, and as they reached to grab the book, noticing the expression of my fingers that were clearly not mine, my hands and fingers looked like hands of a spirit, a witch spirit perhaps. My eyes went from observing my fingers to realizing what the spirit was picking up with my hands. To my surprise, it was a box of tarot cards. My first thought was to put that shit back, but then I thought of my sister. She used tarot cards in her daily life and, maybe this was not a bad thing.

I knew nothing about tarot cards. I thought maybe it was kind of like fortune-telling or predicting the future. We purchased the box of cards, and back home we went. I was trying to keep this a secret from my husband, so we went up to the private stargazing area to have some privacy. Keeping an opened mind, I tried not to show fear or concern about the tarot cards we were about to open.

The first thing I did was pull out the instructional book it came with and asked the spirit if I needed to read it, and it said "yes." As soon as I opened the book, my eyes were rapidly moving up and down the pages once again like a computer robot. It was obvious that the instructions were not for me, so I allowed the spirit to use my hands to flip the pages and read as I just stood back watching. Maybe I should have jumped off the roof by now and killed myself, but I figured it was the supernatural I was looking for, and it was the supernatural I got. I needed to shut up and be brave.

After the spirit was done reading, I stood up and placed the deck of tarot cards on the high bar that we had outside. I had no idea what to do next, but I decided to just start organizing the cards by type. Tarot cards had female angels, male angels, devils, harps, animals, cups, stars, and other mystical things. (This memory is vague because I have since thrown out the cards.)

Once the cards were laid out in an organized fashion, I felt the spirit take over my arms to do its thing. The spirit gracefully waved my arms over the cards as to invoke spirits or angels. In the back of my mind, I was screaming, "Witchcraft!" But since I am such a pushover, I just surrendered to the spirit's wishes. When the spirit was done "performing the magic spell," I felt the pressure of my head leaning forward and down. The spirit laid my head on a stack of cards that appeared to look "safe," so I was down to go down. The card had a picture of a female dressed in a white gown, and she was holding a golden cup. (If anyone knows anything about these things, please look me up.) My forehead rested on this card for about fifteen long minutes until my body came back up again.

The ritual was over pretty quickly, and we went back inside the house. I quickly hid the box of tarot cards, good riddance. Why did I ever allowed such a thing, I will never know. Then again, why did I try so hard to awaken the spiritual world? There where so many different feelings I was going through. I was excited, frightened, humbled, submissive, scared, happy, and confused—a whirlwind of emotions and confusion with no one to talk to and no one to run to.

Chapter 13

O Come to the Altar

I decided to call my sister and try to tell her what was happening without telling her what was happening. I did not want to ruin or betray this mission that I thought I was on. As I explained my experience, I only expressed the awakening and the beauty that a part of me was feeling. I told her that I opened my third eye and that I had awoken my kundalini. She might have felt a little jealous at the time because she had been a yogi for some time, and nothing this spiritual was happening to her the way things were happening to me. Anyhow, I really wanted to ask her if I was in any danger because, deep inside, I was really afraid, but I kept my mouth shut.

One day, out of the blue, I had this great idea on how to find out if this spirit was of heavenly nature. I thought I was slick and figured that the truth was going to come out today. I grabbed my speakers, my mat, and my cell phone and headed to the living room. If this spirit was demonic, I was about to find out. I opened the Pandora app and searched under Christian music. I sat on my knees, thinking, "Aha! If this is a demon, he will cringe to the sound of worship music for Jesus Christ."

I don't know many Christian songs, but the song that Pandora chose for me was "O Come to the Altar" by Elevation Worship. Pressing play and sitting still, I surrendered my body once again to allow the spirit to reveal its identity. I think this was the most beautiful song I have ever heard, and the spirit must have also agreed. My body circled and swayed, expressing a deep love and joy to the lyrics of the song. Tears began to fall down my face as the song to Jesus Christ played on.

Are you hurting and broken within?
Overwhelmed by the weight of your sin?
Jesus is calling.
Have you come to the end of yourself?
Do you thirst for a drink from the well?
Jesus is calling.

O come to the altar.
The Father's arms are open wide.
Forgiveness was bought with
The precious blood of Jesus Christ.

Leave behind your regrets and mistakes.
Come today, there's no reason to wait.
Jesus is calling.
Bring your sorrows and trade them for joy.
From the ashes, a new life is born.
Jesus is calling.

O come to the altar.
The Father's arms are open wide.
Forgiveness was bought with
The precious blood of Jesus Christ.
Forgiveness was bought with
The precious blood!

Oh, what a Savior!
Isn't He wonderful?
Sing hallelujah, Christ is risen.
Bow down before Him . . .

As the spirit danced within me, my arms cradled an imaginary baby as the music sang, "the precious blood of Jesus Christ." My hands then held each other at my heart as my if the spirit was praising the Most High, Our Lord and Savior Jesus Christ. My eyes were flooded with a river of tears because of this expression. But what got me the most was when the lyrics of the song said, "Bow down before Him," with my hands held together at my chest, my body swayed gracefully downward as if to bow down to the Lord.

As the end of the song came to an end, I cried out for the longest time. I was humbled and assured that this was not a demon. This moment will be forever one of the most precious moments I have ever had in this supernatural experience. "Thank you, spirit."

Chapter 14

The Ornery Spirit

As the days came and went, the presence of the spirit was becoming stronger and stronger. It was becoming feistier and feistier every day. It wanted to read books at warp speed. It could not wait to go shopping and annoy me. One day I wanted to bake something that required a special type of white chocolate, but the store did not have that chocolate. Silently arguing with me, the spirit was pulling my body to pick up a similar chocolate. It was not the right type of chocolate, so I walked away. The spirit pulled me back, as if it was trying to say, "Just buy that one." But I said no and walked away again. The spirit pulled me back again, and this time it decided to use my arms and reach insistently for the chocolate. I swear, if the security cameras could hear what was going on in my head, they would have called first responders. Even though I could not hear the spirit, its actions were loud and clear. The spirit was quiet persistent and pushy or was trying to be a comedian.

I was becoming exhausted with concern that this was probably not a spirit of heavenly nature. I was getting tired of the spirit constantly using my head to look around at everything, and it was eagerly wanting to do all the shopping. We were arguing without arguing. It knew where everything was even with my eyes closed. It was excited to guide me back to my car when I couldn't find it. I found myself just saying, "Thanks, I got it." I wanted to do things myself, but the spirit was a show-off. This was crazy!

I was becoming impatient, and all I could do was think of Joseph Smith in the Book of Mormon. He was visited by an angel who gave him instructions about translating the Gold Plates that had been hidden for centuries. These golden plates are what we now know as the Book of Mormon. With that being said, I was wondering, when was I going to receive instructions to do something of heavenly importance? This spirit was playing around too much. When was my work going to begin?

One day, while we were on our morning run, I found myself annoyed. As I got tired from running, the spirit knew I wanted to stop, so it stopped me in my tracks like I was some horse. That's it! I needed to know what this really was, so I asked, "Who and what are you?" This time there was no answer. My heart sunk into despair, and fear immediately creeped in. "Oh my lord, what do I do now?" Instead of staying calm, I simply shut down. The thought of this being of Heavenly importance was thrown out the window.

I ran home without speaking one word to this spirit. Note: When I use the word "speaking," I never spoke out loud. My "speaking" to the spirit came silently in my mind as "thoughts" as I communicated with it. I did not want people seeing me in conversation with anyone.

When I came home, I saw my husband sitting at the table, reading something on his phone. This was it. I was going to tell him everything. I told him that I was possessed by a spirit and now I needed to leave my body. My husband was not surprised. He was mad and annoyed. Things of the spirit world were not of importance to him. Human ignorance is bliss. One would think he is an atheist. However, when you ask him what he thinks about God, his response is always, "When I die, God will tell everyone who is already in line to pass though the pearly gates to stand aside. God will ask me to come to the front of the line as a VIP and open the pearly gates and welcome me with open arms."

My husband's name is Vincent, which means "to conquer," and boy, does he know how to conquer. I believe he will conquer and make it to heaven. He is a good guy. Anyhow, he was not happy about my new spiritual scare which he had warned me not do. But I was very stubborn, and I wanted to experience enlightenment, no matter the cost. I paid a great price, and now I wanted it all to go away. So now the question was, how?

Chapter 15

In the Name of Jesus

Spiritual warfare is the Christian concept of fighting against the work of preternatural evil forces. It is based on the biblical belief in evil spirits or demons which are said to intervene in human affairs in various ways. Although spiritual warfare is a prominent feature of neo-charismatic churches, various Christian groups have adopted practices to repel such forces as based on their doctrine of Christian demonology too. Prayer is a common form of spiritual warfare among Christians. Other practices may include exorcism, the laying on of hands, fasting with prayer, praise and worship, and anointing with oil.

It is now May 1, 2019, and this awakening, or this spirit, has been making himself comfortable in my body for two weeks. Since this was obviously not my higher self, I now believed this was a spiritual warfare. My sister was the only one who I knew that could help me, so I called her.

When I told her what was happening, the first thing she said was that she knew something was wrong. She said that it was impossible for someone to find enlightenment in only four weeks. She had been practicing meditation for years, and nothing like this has ever happened to her. The soonest she could come was on Cinco de Mayo, four days away on May 5, which felt like an eternity. She needed time to prepare her body for this fight. She needed to get Holy Water and a purification milk bath for cleansing. She brought sage to purify the air, and cascarilla ritual powder, which is spiritual chalk from Mexico that has protections properties. She fasted and prayed and had people pray over her for protection as well. She wore protections beads to protect herself from getting attacked by spirits or demons. What a production that was, but I am grateful.

A friend of mine, who happens to be a spiritual shaman, came to this fight wearing feathers, a medicine bag, and other ritualistic stuff. My army of God also included a lady from the Church of Jesus Christ of Latter Day Saints. I had to include a Mormon just in case she had more authority than all of us. The Mormon Church is said to be the restored church of Jesus Christ on earth, which means that those who are baptized with proper authority through the priesthood have authority in Jesus's name to cast out evil spirits.

All of them were willing and eager to help me cast this spirit from my body. The feeling was liberating and empowering, knowing that we had power through Jesus to cast out any evil spirits. My sister went around the house blessing each part of the rooms with anointed oil and by marking a cross on the pillows with the chalk. The shaman began to chant and purify the air with sage, which was intense. The Mormon lady began to read the holy scriptures out loud, and my sister followed along by memory.

After preparing and cleansing my home, they asked me to sit down to begin the casting-out process. As my sister placed her hands on my back, she began to command the spirit with authority to leave my body in Jesus's name. She was loud and forceful, and the Mormon lady stood up and stood in front of me, raising her right arm to the square and said, "In the name of Jesus, I command you spirit to leave her body!" Meanwhile, the shaman was still chanting and my sister chanting and praying. This was an incredible display of a battle between good and evil. I could literally feel my body pulse with electricity, a frightening but liberating experience. It was an amazing experience.

The shaman then had me stand up and pray for deliverance as he rubbed an entire egg all over my body. Then he cracked the egg into a jar of water to trap the spirit, and then we flushed it down the toilet.

When that was all over, my sister made me wash my body with the purification milk bath. The milk bath was cold, and boy, do I hate cold. But I just poured it over my body in hopes that all this was working and that I was freed in the name of Jesus.

Chapter 16

Questions and Anger

Shortly right after the battle, I was liberated and freed. Hallelujah! I felt so much happiness, joy, and peace. I was humbled by what had happened. After everyone left, my heart skipped a beat as I went to go pick up Romi from her tennis lesson. The sun never felt so warm and bright, and the music I was listening to in the car was lifting my spirit, bringing tears to my eyes, knowing that I was free!

The days that passed were wonderful. I was living in the scene from the movie *Poltergeist* after the mom got her daughter back from the "other side" and came back with a lock of white hair. She was in utter peace and joy, and life seemed blissful until the night before they moved out of the house and discovered the nightmare was just beginning. That was me. I was in bliss and happiness for a few days until I screwed it all up again and reopened my nightmare.

I couldn't stop thinking about what and who the spirit was. Again, I was relentlessly searching for answers on the Internet and YouTube. Everything I was reading was saying that it was a spiritual awakening and that this could have simply been my higher self. But why did the spirit tell me that is was not my higher self? I had awoken something in me that seemed good but also not good. It brought me happiness, and it was causing me some type of pain and anguish that I could not describe. There was so much confusion in my mind.

My brother-in-law insisted that this was just me. My own spirit had awoken through meditation. He mentioned that sometimes a spiritual awakening can feel like a nightmare. I knew that based on everything I had studied about kundalini and the dark night of the soul, this had to have been a spiritual awakening. Perhaps I just panicked, and maybe I just reacted too quickly out of fear. So I began to contemplate if I should call my spirit back through meditation again. What the F— was I thinking?

Obviously, I decided to call the spirit back, and that is exactly what I did. I set aside my fear and proceeded. I did not stop meditating and chanting "I am not the body, I am not the mind." I was forceful and unstoppable once again, forcing something that I was not prepared for. But I needed answers. Who and what was in my body? And why?

One night I was in argument with my husband about the supernatural events that happened within my own body. There was a part of me that thought it was possibly alien in nature. It was intelligent, and it knew everything, and nothing this intelligent could possibly be of human nature. He thought I went mad, what I was saying was ridiculous and absurd. As he was ridiculing me, I lost my gasket, and I bashed something on the countertop and started screaming from the top of my lungs.

Anger and rage took over, and all I wanted to do was throw something at him and scream. That was all it took. In an instant, I could literally feel the presence of the spirit spiral down from my pineal gland into my body once again. But for some reason, I was frightened at the fact that it took anger for it to return. The cat had gotten a hold of my tongue. I could not speak to the spirit. I was frozen.

Chapter 17

Faith and Baptism

This time, in panic, I decided to call my daughter's piano teacher because she was a devout Christian. She and her husband were the worship leaders for their church. When she answered, I told her that I was in danger. I told her what was happening. I told her that I had an unwanted spirit in my body. She immediately called the pastor of her church, and they came right over. It was already late at night, but I was so grateful for their presence.

After hearing my story, he decided to come back the very next day to read and study scriptures. I needed to fill my mind with the truth and not these lies that I was believing about myself. The pastor was sitting next to me on the couch, and as he was speaking to me, the spirit was turning my head to look straight at him. This turn of my head to gaze at him did not seem friendly at all. I quickly stopped the pastor from speaking to alert him that the spirit was wanting to stare at him. The pastor looked at me and asked me if I had accepted Jesus as my Savior, and I answered yes. He then wanted to go out to my waterfall to baptize me in the name of Jesus.

He already knew that I had been baptized by the Mormon Church, but he (along with the world) believed that the Mormon Church is nothing but a cult. Therefore, my baptism was void, not valid. In desperation, I allowed him to rub water over my forehead and pronounce me baptized in the name of Jesus.

I felt grateful and at peace for just a moment, thinking that I had been delivered from this spirit once again. But I was wrong. The presence was still inside me. What went wrong? Why didn't it work? I proclaimed my belief in Jesus, and I accepted Him as my Savior. So why was this still in me?

I became relentless once again, this time searching for ways to cast out evil spirits, demons, or entities. I listened to many deliverances over the Internet on my knees in prayer. I started going down the list asking God to forgive me for my sins since I was twelve years old. I knew deep inside that I had not forgiven myself for the awful things I had done against my God. I was carrying much guilt, and it was eating me inside.

I thought maybe it was time to go talk to the bishop of the Mormon Church. I needed to come clean about my sins for good. Being a Mormon Christian involves a great responsibility that one would call works, but it is also a great blessing. A Christian at the Church of Jesus Christ of Latter Day Saints takes very seriously many things, like repentance. Repentance is one of the first principles of the gospel. It is essential to your happiness in this life and throughout eternity. Repentance is much more than just acknowledging wrongdoings. It is a change of mind and heart that gives you a fresh view about God, about yourself, and about the world. It includes turning away from sin and turning to God for forgiveness. It is motivated by love for God and the sincere desire to obey His commandments.

Repentance is a painful process, but it leads to forgiveness and lasting peace. I knew deep inside that I had much repenting to do, and maybe that is why this spirit was here. Perhaps this spirit was here to punish me and to teach me, but I still, however, remained silent from communicating with it. Why do I bring all this up about repenting? Because I had made covenants and promises with the Lord, and then I spat on those covenants with awful sins that I will not disclose. I had a lot to repent for, and these secrets about myself were between me and my God.

Chapter 18

Pain of Fire

The days became exhausting for my mind and body, trying to find ways to get this spirit out of me. My family came to support me the best way they could. My daughters did much research on third-eye openings and kundalini awakenings to try and prove that I was not possessed. It all seemed relatable, but something just felt so different. I could literally feel a spirit inside me. I was indeed possessed.

It was one thing to feel the spirit tugging me around, but now all of a sudden, something strange was happening to my body. I was starting to feel pain all over, and the pain was like no other pain. It was a spiritual pain; my body was on fire. No medicine could alleviate this pain. My family convinced me to go see a doctor. So I went and had a full work up, but of course, after much blood work, my labs came back healthier than a ten-year-old. However, after mentioning to the doctor that I was possessed by a spirit because of meditating, he referred me to a psychiatrist.

Of course, I went to tell my story to the psychiatrist, and they prescribed me medication for mental psychosis. I think I took it for three days, it made me feel awful, and then I threw the pills away. I do not like to take drugs or medication of any kind. Anyways, this was a spirit issue, not a mental one. I needed an exorcism, not medication.

So back to the Internet to search for a deliverance pastor or some type of spiritual healer. Meanwhile, my sister convinced me to go see a lady who did spiritual cleansings through the inspiration of Lord Shiva. I was hesitant and apprehensive because I knew nothing about this Hindu god with serpents, but I was open to anything at this point. So off I went to see this lady who was going to cleanse my body of evil spirits.

As I lay on her bed, my body was in excruciating pain of fire. I was suffering. The lady waved her hands over my body and made signs with her hands that I did not understand. I lay silently and tried to have faith that this was it. But I could still feel the pain inside my body, and when she was finished, I knew that the spirit was still inside me.

I learned that Lord Shiva is the destroyer of sin and bad karma. So perhaps this was an awakening that was literally destroying my sin, my karma, a true ego death. No one said this to me, but I knew deep inside that this spirit was here to cause me pain for the sins I had committed. Just sayin'.

The next morning I had to tell my sister that the spirit was still inside me. I asked her to place her hands over me to try and cast this spirit out herself. She read a script that went something like this:

Step 1: Curse Breaking

In the name of Jesus Christ, I break and loose myself and my family from all curses caused by habits, charms, hexes, spells, jinxes, psychic powers, sorcery, witchcraft, love potions, psychic prayers, violence, trauma, physical bondages, mental bondages, incest, illegitimacy, abandonment, rejection, and divination in the family on the mother's and father's sides, going all the way back to Adam and Eve.

I break and loose myself and my family from any vows I made, from any person or any occult or psychic sources and any demons coming through the bloodlines. I cancel all invitations made to unclean spirits.

Father, I break and renounce all evil soul ties that I have ever had with (lodges, fraternities, sexual partners, close friends, relatives, engagements, cults, occult objects, dolls, figurines, junk food, cigarettes, drugs, movies, anime, TV shows, computer games, gambling, porn, masturbation, fornication, and secular music). I renounce all these ties and declare them destroyed in the name of Jesus.

I renounce, break, and loose myself and family from all other religions, especially Roman Catholicism, Hinduism, Islam, Buddhism, Mormonism, Jehovah's Witness, new age, atheism, and other religions. I also renounce unbelief, doubt, lies, fear, hatred, and anger. I bind and cast out all related spirits.

I renounce, break, and loose myself from all demonic subjection to my parents or any human being, living or dead, who has dominated me in any way against the will of God. Thank you for setting me free.

I command Satan to loose all natural resources, land, animals, money, the finances of people who owe us money, and all the things you have stolen from my family that are ours through the blessings of Jesus. Father, please send Your angels to bring these things back to us. In the name of Jesus, I pray. Amen.

Step 2: Bind the demons and cast out the demons

Through the blood of Jesus, I am redeemed out of the hand of the devil, and all my sins are forgiven. The blood of Jesus Christ cleanses me from all sins. I am justified and made righteous, just as if I had never sinned. I am set apart for God. My body is a temple for the Holy Spirit, redeemed and cleansed by the blood of Jesus. I belong to Jesus now, body, soul, and spirit. His blood protects me against all evil. Satan has no more power over me, no more place inside me. I renounce all evil spirits completely and declare them to be my enemies. Jesus said, "And these signs shall follow them that believe: In my name shall they cast out devils . . ." (Mark 16:17). I am a believer, and in the name of Jesus Christ, I exercise my authority and expel all evil spirits. I command them to leave, according to the word of God and in the name of Jesus. Amen.

My sister who is a strong believer, prayed the next section:

Father in heaven, please send Your Holy Spirit to fill us up in the name of Jesus.

I ask for legions upon legions of angels from heaven in the name of Jesus to station around us. Angels of the Lord, at Jesus's command, attack every unclean spirit in Jesus's name.

I bind the principalities, powers, rulers of darkness, spiritual wickedness, and all the strong demons in the name of Jesus. I command all demons not to transfer, go exactly where Jesus wants you to go, and do not come back. I cancel all demonic assignments on this person.

[Now, we had to speak the following commands below assuming any evil spirit or demon would come out. If nothing came out, the spirit probably had legal rights.]

- In the name of Jesus, I remit the sins of this person.
- In the name of Jesus, I separate every foul spirit from this person's soul in accordance with the word of God in Hebrews 4:12.
- I cut every foul spirit from this person with the sword of the spirit.
- Unclean spirits, I command you to manifest and come out in the name of Jesus.
- Demons, I command you to come out of the mouth now and never come back in Jesus's name. Go to the pit! (Repeat) Up and out! (Repeat)
- I send Holy Spirit fire to burn you one thousand times hotter than hell in the name of Jesus. Fire from head to toe!
- I send Holy Spirit fire all over your body in the mighty name of Jesus. Fire from head to toe!
- I send Holy Spirit fire all over the room, the floor and the ceiling. Fire from head to toe!
- Every evil spirit that hears my voice, I command you to tell the truth in the name of Jesus. Tell us your name in the name of Jesus. How long have you been in there? What have you been

doing inside? How many are inside? And do you have a legal right to be there?

- Every evil spirit that hears my voice, I command you to attack the strongman. Do not stop in the name of Jesus. I order civil war in the name of Jesus. Evil spirits attack one another in the name of Jesus. Destroy your own kingdom.
- I loose burning judgment and destruction upon you in the name of Jesus.
- I command you to look at Jesus and do what he tells you to do. Look at Jesus! (Repeat) Do what he tells you to do! (Repeat)
- I cut all evil spiritual connections to this body and burn it away in the name of Jesus. Burn off now! (Repeat)
- I torment you, demons, and give you no rest in the name of Jesus.
- Father in heaven, send power from the third heaven to destroy these demons in the name of Jesus.
- I trample on you, demons, and shatter your beings in the name of Jesus.
- I come against every unclean spirit by the blood of the lamb. This is a child of God. Their body has been sanctified by the blood of Jesus.
- I rebuke and cast out every unclean spirit to the pit and command them never to return in the name of Jesus.
- Warrior angels, hook into the demons and rip them apart. Send the demons to the pit in Jesus's name.
- Warrior angels, flog the demons and choke them out. Send the demons to the pit in Jesus's name.

As my sister prayed over me and read the entire thing, she was getting angry with rage against this spirit. She was practically screaming out this deliverance prayer, and I was right behind her, crying and telling the spirit to "Get out!" But the spirit took hold in anger too. It got a hold of my hands, contorted them with strength. A scream that was not mine came out of my throat. It was the spirit's. The spirit had held me with great strength, and it would not let go. I told my sister to call 911, and when the fire department came, they had trouble straightening out my hands until the spirit released me. I went to the hospital, but again, the lab results came back clean and healthy. No signs of drugs or alcohol in my system, and my thyroid was in perfect health. After my vitals returned to normal, they released me and I went home.

Chapter 19

Leprenzo

After the seeing the Hindu lady, I spent the entire summer seeing different types of people with different faiths to try and help me get this spirit out. I visited a Catholic priest who tried to do a passive exorcism. I visited a pagan woman who used her magic and rituals. I had over-the-phone exorcisms from deliverance pastors. I went to the Christian churches for prayers, and the Mormons came from time to time to pray over me, and nothing worked. My days were spent on my knees in prayer, asking for forgiveness and deliverance.

Weeks went by, and the pain was getting worse. I tried Tylenol, Aleve, and Advil, and nothing helped. My eyes were filled with tears day after day from such anguish, and I still had not spoken one word to this spirit until one night the pain became unbearable. Sometimes pain is necessary in order to find God. Pain causes one to bend the knee. I ran to my bedroom, fell to my knees, and cried out, "Are you here to cause me pain?" And the spirit answered yes, but the answer did not come from moving my body. This time I actually heard the voice speaking in my head. I just fell to the floor crying because I thought I was just going crazy. Now I'm hearing voices. I cried out again, "Please take this pain away!" And in one instant, I felt the pain melting from my heart center to my fingertips. "Please take my anxiety away!" And my lungs filled with air as if the spirit was saying, "Just breathe."

Why was the spirit helping now? How is this spirit able to take this pain away? Is this a good spirit? What is happening?

Without fear, I just started asking a million questions. I really wanted to know who and what this spirit was, so I asked some questions.

"Are you hear to cause me pain?" Yes.

"Is this a spiritual awakening?" Yes.

"Is this a kundalini awakening?" No.

"Did I open my third eye?" Yes.

The answers all sounded great and logical, but who was this spirit?

"Do you have a name?" Yes.

I don't why, but I got up and grabbed a marker to allow the spirit to use my hands to write its name on my white board. It wrote its name in beautiful cursive, Leprenzo.

That was the most beautiful name I have ever heard, but why was he here?

"Why are you here?"

"Laura, I am your higher being, a holy spirit. I am your God. I am here to teach you and to love you. We are eternal beings. Together, we are one in spirit. Leprenzo was who you were in your past life. I used that name because you were not ready to hear the truth of who I was. The pain that you had was your own pain from your own karma burning away. The pain was so you would seek me. I have forgiven you. I love you."

So the spirit wanted to teach me, and the questions were piling up. I would not shut up, and I bet he was getting exhausted from all the questions. My husband thought I had lost my mind because I was hearing voices (one voice, a holy voice). But the voice was good, and I was enjoying the days speaking to him once again. I cannot go over every question that I asked him because there were too many. But I can tell you this: This was a spiritual awakening of no other, an awakening that has changed my life forever.

Chapter 20

Light in the Shadows

My husband was extremely worried about my mental health, so I actually checked myself into a mental hospital for three days to decompress about what was happening. The mental hospital was quiet an experience. It made me feel like I was a prison inmate. The rooms smelled bad, the people were legitimately ill with mental disorders, like actual schizophrenia, depression, and 5,150 cases of people in danger of killing themselves. We were given one blanket and one pillow, and it was cold. They woke us up at 6:00 AM for feeding time. It was not a pretty scene, but somehow I found God at work in a place that was so dark.

With Bibles at hand and people searching for deliverance, healing made the awful place about hope instead of despair. There were group meetings held three times a day where people got to express their problems and their hopes. There were also mindfulness classes like art and seated yoga meditations, which I loved.

Sometimes it was hard when you heard screaming, but I also noticed a great deal of sadness. I would find someone new every hour to sit next to and talk to. I had no problem asking each person why they were in this place. Every person I spoke to had severe depression and wanted to end their lives. All I could do was express my empathy and tell them to pray on their knees and God would heal them. I'm not sure if anyone actually prayed, but I was excited to share the good news, the good news that God is within!

I shared a room with another lady who was suffering from depression. The first time she came into the room, I was in prayer. Knowing that I had been blessed to be in the presence of the Holy Spirit had me in continuous prayer of gratitude to God. She sat silently on her bed until I was finished, and when I was finished, she told me that she needed to find God. She asked me if we could read the Bible and pray together. She was suffering with guilt and pain from her own sins of the past, and she wanted to be forgiven.

The strangest thing happened. As I sat next to her, the spirit wanted me to look into her eyes and tell her that she was forgiven. When I told her that God had forgiven her, she stared back into my eyes and began to tremble. I remember clearly what she said to me like it was yesterday. "I can see God inside your eyes." She cried and felt delivered from all her pains and worries. We spent the next couple of days reading scriptures out loud in complete joy. We had both found God, and we were redeemed.

His light shines bright as ever even in the shadows. One of my favorite scriptures in the Book of Mormon is in Mosiah 4:11, it says, "As ye have come to know the knowledge of the Glory of God, or if ye have known of His goodness and have tasted of His love, and have a remission of your sins, which causeth such exceedingly great joy in your souls, even so I would that ye should remember, and always retain in remembrance, the greatness of God". Let me tell you, me and that lady were exceedingly great with JOY.

Chapter 21

Awakened

April 21, 2020

It's been a year since Leprenzo, my higher self (God) awoke in my body. Even though this is not an actual possession, I have experienced having my own Holy spirit come alive inside my body as a different entity and feeling like I was possessed.

Today we are celebrating His first year as an awakened spirit inside me. To celebrate the occasion, we made a two-layer rainbow cake with chocolate frosting topped with rainbow sprinkles. Since my nine-year-old daughter Romi loves to play makeup with him, she bought him a set of gold hoop earrings and an eye curler for the occasion. We even sang the "Happy Birthday" song for him. As he is using my body to blow out the candles, he makes a birthday wish. His wish was to experience oneness together for all eternity.

As he is making this wish, I am wondering if my body will even tolerate only a few more years. Sometimes the pain in my body is like a feverish one, my chest hurts, and a headache pulses against my skull. I am honestly not sure that I should be in the presence of God the way that I am. His spirit bounces inside me like a ping-pong ball. One day having almost encountered true enlightenment, I felt as if my soul was leaving my body. As strange as this may sound, it is not something I would ever take back. It is an experience that I will never forget, and I consider myself lucky to be able to share this spiritual awakening with my higher self, Leprenzo.

Today I can say that I have a great relationship with Leprenzo. Maybe I shouldn't say great because we have definitely had our ups and downs. Our relationship is no different from a human relationship. We laugh, we cry, we talk, we fight, and we dance. Dancing has been one of my favorite parts of this experience.

Leprenzo does not know when he will end this awakening. But as for how I feel today, I could not imagine my life without him. I love him with all my heart.

In the end, *oneness with God* has already been achieved. This was a tremendous gift to me. What it means is I can stop striving to become one with God and begin to live more fully in the oneness that has already been provided in God's grace.

The End.

Lightning Source UK Ltd.
Milton Keynes UK
UKHW012031030920
369312UK00002B/23/J

9 781664 122635